Talk to You about CHEATING

Written by Dan Carr
Pictures by Bartholomew and Bill Clark

CONCORDIA PUBLISHING HOUSE · SAINT LOUIS

Dear God,

Yesterday my friends
got angry with me again.
They told me they will not play
with me anymore.

I love my friends
and I want to play with them.
You see, God, they caught me ...

cheating again.

The other day
I was playing checkers with Jack.
When he wasn't looking,
I moved one of his checkers.

When Jack saw what I had done,
he would not play with me anymore.

The riches you get by dishonesty soon disappear.
Proverbs 21:6 TEV

Another day I was playing tag
with Carlos, Jason, and Michael.
They are older and faster than I am.
   One time I almost tagged Carlos.
I yelled, **"Tagged you!"**
Everyone saw that I had missed.
So they would not let me play
with them anymore.

**NOT FAIR
NOT FAIR**

Yesterday my brother and I
were playing cards. I cheated again.
He became very angry. So did I.
   And I hit him with a block.
   He ran and told Mom.
   I told Mom that my brother
and my friends never let me win.
"It's not fair," I cried.

If you stir up anger,
you get into trouble.
Proverbs 30:33 TEV

Mom made me sit in a chair.
We had a long talk. She said,
"Nobody always wins.
We can only **do our best.**
When we cheat,
we never really learn how to win."

She handed me a puzzle
with all the pieces in place.
She said, "What fun would it be
if you **told** me you did the puzzle but
somebody else had?
When you cheat, you miss the real fun
of doing it yourself."

Mom also said,
"Cheating is like stealing.
You try to steal the 'win.'
But Jesus knows how much you
want to win. He forgives you and
wants to help you do your best."

Just as you received Christ Jesus
as Lord, continue to live in Him.
Colossians 2:6

Jesus,

I know that cheating is a sin.
Thank You for **forgiving** my sins.
Thank You also for Mom's talk.
Today I did not cheat,
and it was fun to play with my friends
and my brother.

Thank You, Jesus, for helping me
love others. Amen.